Bb Clarinet / Bb Tenor Saxophone

Audio Access Included

Instrumental Solos for Worship

Arranged by James Curnow

Contents

PLAYBACK+
Speed • Pitch • Balance • Loop

To access audio, visit:
www.halleonard.com/mylibrary

Enter Code
5130-7781-8725-5912

ISBN 978-90-431-0979-6

M U S I C

EXCLUSIVELY DISTRIBUTED BY

HAL•LEONARD®

Visit Hal Leonard Online at
www.halleonard.com

Contact us:
Hal Leonard
7777 West Bluemound Road
Milwaukee, WI 53213
Email: info@halleonard.com

In Europe, contact:
Hal Leonard Europe Limited
42 Wigmore Street
Marylebone, London, W1U 2RN
Email: info@halleonardeurope.com

In Australia, contact:
Hal Leonard Australia Pty. Ltd.
4 Lentara Court
Cheltenham, Victoria, 3192 Australia
Email: info@halleonard.com.au

Great Hymns

INTRODUCTION

This collection of some of the world's greatest hymns was created for, and is dedicated to, my good friend and musical colleague, Philip Smith, Principal Trumpet, New York Philharmonic Orchestra. The goal of these arrangements is to allow instrumentalists the opportunity to give praise and adoration to God through their musical abilities.

Though the arrangements have been written for trumpet, with Phil in mind, cued notes have been added to allow players at many different levels and on various instruments to perform them. They are also playable on all instruments (C treble clef, Bb Treble Clef, Eb, F or Bass Clef) by simply purchasing the appropriate book that coincides with the key of their instrument.

The piano accompaniment book has been written to work with all instruments, or an accompaniment track for each hymn is included with the online audio, should a piano accompanist not be available. Appropriate tuning notes have also been added to allow the soloists the opportunity to adjust their intonation to the intonation of the recorded accompaniment.

May you enjoy using this collection and find it useful in extending your musical ministry.

Kindest regards,

James Curnow
President
Curnow Music Press, Inc.

Audio performed by Becky Shaw - Piano, Michael Rintamaa - Organ

Dedicated to Philip Smith, Principal Trumpet, New York Philharmonic Orchestra

ALL CREATURES OF OUR GOD AND KING

Lasst Uns Erfreuen

Arr. **James Curnow** (ASCAP)

Bb Clarinet, Bb Tenor Saxophone

Dedicated to Philip Smith, Principal Trumpet, New York Philharmonic Orchestra

PRAISE TO THE LORD, THE ALMIGHTY
Lobe Den Herren

Arr. **James Curnow** (ASCAP)

Dedicated to Philip Smith, Principal Trumpet, New York Philharmonic Orchestra

BE THOU MY VISION
Slane

Arr. **James Curnow** (ASCAP)

B♭ Clarinet, B♭ Tenor Saxophone

Dedicated to Philip Smith, Principal Trumpet, New York Philharmonic Orchestra
O WORSHIP THE KING
Lyons

Arr. **James Curnow** (ASCAP)

JOYFUL, JOYFUL, WE ADORE THEE

Dedicated to Philip Smith, Principal Trumpet, New York Philharmonic Orchestra

Hymn to Joy

Arr. James Curnow (ASCAP)

Bb Clarinet, Bb Tenor Saxophone

Dedicated to Philip Smith, Principal Trumpet, New York Philharmonic Orchestra

BRETHREN, WE HAVE MET TO WORSHIP
Holy Manna Variations

Arr. **James Curnow** (ASCAP)

Dedicated to Philip Smith, Principal Trumpet, New York Philharmonic Orchestra

WE GATHER TOGETHER
Kremser

Arr. **James Curnow** (ASCAP)

Bb Clarinet, Bb Tenor Saxophone

Dedicated to Philip Smith, Principal Trumpet, New York Philharmonic Orchestra

I SING THE MIGHTY POWER OF GOD

Ellacombe

Arr. **James Curnow** (ASCAP)

Dedicated to Philip Smith, Principal Trumpet, New York Philharmonic Orchestra

A MIGHTY FORTRESS IS OUR GOD

Ein' Feste Burg

Arr. **James Curnow** (ASCAP)

Bb Clarinet, Bb Tenor Saxophone

ALL HAIL THE POWER
Coronation, Diadem, Miles Lane

Arr. **James Curnow** (ASCAP)